WARTIME WWII MILITARY RECORDS ON COMFORT WOMEN

Compilation of U.S./Allied/Dutch/Japanese Military Documents

Archie Miyamoto
Lieutenant Colonel, U.S. Army, Retired
2d Edition, April 2017

INTRODUCTION

This compilation of extracts from wartime military documents during and immediately after WWII provides unbiased primary source information related to comfort women. It includes:

- U.S./Allied wartime interrogation reports of Japanese soldiers, comfort women and comfort station operators.

- Military translations of captured documents.

- War crimes trials records related to comfort women.

- Excerpts from a Dutch government study on recruitment of prostitutes in the Dutch East Indies and Dutch military interrogation reports.

- Australian Records of War Crimes trials.

- Japanese foreign ministry and military documents, including handwritten unit journals and regulations related to the issue.

- Original Korean records. This includes an analysis by a Korean professor of a diary of a Korean manager of a comfort station in Burma and in Singapore.

The purpose of this compilation is neither to defend nor condemn Japan's use of the comfort women system. Prostitution was legal at the time and that is a separate issue. This compilation is to determine the scope and nature of the comfort women system and the volunteer or involuntary status of the women. These original documents provide detailed, objective evidence on these questions. Most of the original reports are lengthy and cover material not related to the comfort women issue. Only relevant sections are quoted. Salient points are highlighted in bold letters.

This compilation is by no means complete and research continues. The military records in this compilation are public domain and therefore free to use by anyone without permission. Copies of documents can be obtained from national archives and other sources. The WAM museum (Women's Active Museum in War and Peace), a non-governmental museum in Tokyo, which condemns Japan's use of the comfort women system, has a wealth of Japanese, U.S. and Dutch documents. Its web site is: http://wam-peace.org/koubunsho/index.html.

Attributions are omitted for many of the general comments by the author since they are not considered germane or are common knowledge. The data in the military documents speak for themselves.

TABLE OF CONTENTS

A. BACKGROUND INFORMATION ON THE COMFORT WOMEN ISSUE

Japan is accused of abducting 200,000 women, mostly from Korea, during WWII for its comfort women system. These original documents from WWII reveal the true nature of the comfort women system and provide a totally different perspective. At the same time, it raises questions about why these unproven allegations are brought to the United States. Delving into that will be left to others and only a brief explanation is provided in this introductory chapter and in the concluding remarks. Cursory background information on the relationship between Korea and Japan is provided to assist in understanding why these two nations which are so close in so many ways are so far apart.

It was common knowledge the Japanese military controlled the association of its troops with prostitutes utilizing what was referred to as a comfort women system and regulated the conduct of brothel owners, prostitutes, and also soldiers. The allegation that the women were abducted sex slaves did not arise until decades after the end of WWII.

Comfort stations offered various amenities other than prostitutes. Those with prostitutes were referred to as special comfort stations. Most of the women came from Korea and Japan. Some were from Taiwan and China. In many instances, local brothels were also authorized for use by the troops. In Japanese records, these authorized local brothels were sometimes referred to as comfort stations, at other times as "brothels" and the women as "prostitutes." These authorized brothels were required to comply with regulatory standards similar to those of comfort stations.

The ostensible reason given in the sex slave narrative is that it is about the exploitation of women. This generates sympathy and support, but other than allegations there has been little presentation of original documentation. During WWII, the existence of comfort women was common knowledge and cases of involuntary recruitment of women were prosecuted as war crimes. The U.S. prosecuted one incident in Guam involving two women who were verbally but not physically coerced into becoming prostitutes by a resident Japanese, the Dutch a few cases of involuntary prostitution by soldiers in Indonesia, Australia none. Those alleging 200,000 women were abducted for sex slaves have not explained how that could be kept a secret for decades after WWII, especially since involuntary recruitment was considered a war crime and the few known cases prosecuted. To imply Allied authorities, during over six years of war crimes investigations, failed to uncover the other 200,000 is an insult to the integrity and competence of U.S. and Allied authorities.

Since Korea was part of the Japanese Empire during WWII, it was not a party to the 1951 San Francisco Peace Treaty formally ending WWII. In 1965, the Normalization Treaty between Korea and Japan settled all grievances between the two nations "completely and finally." Japan provided $800 million in payment, loans, and assets (equal to billions in today's dollars). All issues were considered settled.

Many decades later, instead of seeking redress from the Korean government which had been compensated by Japan in settlement of all issues, Korean comfort women claims were directed against Japan. Since under the bilateral treaty all issues had been settled, the Japanese government had no obligation to pay the women but out of sympathy for the suffering and hardship endured by the women for Japan, encouraged private donations from the Japanese people. In 1994, the Asian Women's Fund, a fund raiser supported by the Japanese government, was established. It raised and paid millions to all known former comfort women of all nations. In addition to this, a number of Japanese officials, including prime ministers, made apologies time and again to resolve the issue but protests continued. None of the apologies admitted to abduction. In December, 2015, the governments of Korea and Japan agreed the issue has been "finally and irreversibly" resolved with Japan paying $8.3 million to former Korean comfort women. Yet, protests in Korea continue unabated with even talk of abrogating the agreement. The Korean government appears powerless to bring closure.

It is no secret that Chong Dae Hyup, the main South Korean organization behind this issue, has ties to North Korea. This campaign is also supported by some Japanese who thrive on exaggerating the sins of Japan. Most Americans see this simply as a women's issue and are quick to provide support. The allegations are believable because of the many atrocities committed by Japanese troops during WWII.

There are many who do not know what to believe without evidence to prove or disprove the allegations. Hopefully, this compilation will serve to clarify the issue. For those who understand the political motives driving this issue, this compilation will hopefully be of some assistance. Explaining the activities of the China lobby in the U.S. and the information war taking place is outside the scope of this compilation.

The claim of 200,000 abducted sex slaves have relied on historians and others quoting secondary source material or isolated cases of a handful of victims of involuntary prostitution Testimonies of former comfort women regarding forced recruitment or abduction have not been substantiated by witness statements, police reports, or other corroborating evidence. With 200,000 alleged victims, thousands of corroborating evidence should exist. Even if testimonies of former comfort women are factual, they do not constitute evidence of 200,000 abductions for sex slaves by the Japanese military.

Some knowledge of the annexation period of Korea by Japan is essential in understanding the anti-Japan sentiments of Koreans that keeps this issue alive. If one understands the true history of the period, it will raise serious doubt whether the abduction of Korean women by the Japanese military could have taken place. Without knowing this background and the differing view of this period by Koreans and the Japanese, it will not be possible to comprehend the true nature of the comfort women issue and why it remains such an almost insurmountable obstacle in friendly relations between the two nations.

Korea was annexed by Japan in 1910. For ten years prior to that it had been a protectorate of Japan. Considerable expenditures were made by Japan to bring Korea into the 20th century. Today, many Koreans, and Americans too, regard the annexation by

Japan as the most brutal colonization in history because that is what they have been taught since the end of WWII.

An objective reference is former University of Chicago Professor Alleyne Ireland's <u>The New Korea</u> (E.P. Dutton &Co., 1926), which gives a detailed description of the annexation period. The following are a few excerpts from his book.

"My opinion of the Japanese administration in Korea has been derived from...what I saw..., what I read..., and from discussions with persons (Japanese, Korean and foreign) who were living in the Peninsula at the time of my visit.

"It is true that at the time Japan annexed Korea in 1910, the actual condition of life in the Peninsula were extremely bad. This was not due any lack of inherent intelligence and ability in the Korean, but to the stupidity and corruption which had characterized the government of the Korean dynasty, and due to the existence of a royal court which maintained a system of licensed cruelty and corruption throughout Korea. Such was the misrule under which Koreans had suffered for generations after generations that all incentive to industry and social progress had been destroyed...."

"The New Korea of which I write is a Korea which has developed under the wise and sympathetic guidance of Governor-General Saito. At the time of my own visit to Korea in 1922, the Governor-General had nearly completed three years of his tenure in the office. The following is the list of measures...."

" 1. Non-discrimination between Japanese and Korean officials.
*   2. Simplification of laws and regulations.*
*   3. Prompt transaction of state business.*
*   4. Decentralization policy.*
*   5. Improvement of local organizations.*
*   6. Respect for native culture and customs.*
*   7. Freedom of speech, meeting, and press.*
*   8. Spread of education and development of industry.*
*   9. Re-organizing of the police system.*
*   10. Enlargement of medical and sanitary agencies.*
*   11. Guidance of the people.*
*   12. Advancement of men of talent.*
*   13. Friendly feeling between Japanese and Koreans."*

"The general consensus of opinion in Korea in 1922 was that Governor-General Saito...had accomplished notable reforms, that in the matter of education he had ministered very generously to the cultural ambitions of the people, and in regard to their political ambitions he had shown himself eager to foster local self-government and to infuse a spirit of friendliness and cooperation into the personal relations of the Japanese and Koreans."

Professor Atul Kohli of Princeton, in <u>State Directed Development</u> (<u>Political Power and Industrialization in the Global Periphery</u>), (2004), in the section on Korea states that the average life span of Koreans during Japanese annexation rose from 23 years to 45, population doubled, and industrial output increased tenfold.

Since the end of WWII, Koreans have refused to acknowledge anything positive about this period of history. Recently, retired Korean general/diplomat Choe Kyung-rok had this to say about the annexation period and Korean attitude. The site, (http://earlgrey2341.blog.fc2.com/blog-entry-367.html), is translated below:

"That Japan, during the annexation period due to making large investments, enabled Korea to go in one leap from a miserable situation into modernization, is a reality that no matter what cannot be denied. After annexation, Japan began large scale public projects beginning with railroads, roads,...forestry, control of rivers, dam construction, and construction of school facilities. As a result, up to that time in Korea, there were multitudes of starving jobless people, but jobs became available for common citizens and many thrived. Japan corrected the careless governance of the final Lee Dynasty and created a Korean society of law.

"During the time Japan governed Korea, that Japan conducted one-way exploitation greatly contradicts reality. Today, those knowledgeable Koreans who experienced that period of annexation, while they know that is the reality, refuse to recognize that objective reality.

"Korea, due to the efforts of Japan, was able to in a short period, adopt the Japanese system of pragmatism learned from the West, and enter the modern world. With the advent of Japanese rule, many Koreans for the first time were able to reap the benefits of their labor. Also, public welfare of Koreans increased dramatically.

"Even if one is a Korean, although small in numbers, there are those who objectively acknowledge reality, with proper acknowledgment of facts, are able to evaluate the annexation period. However, these people of conscience are very few, and by creating a false history by national design and forcing an anti-Japan policy, we are today an irretrievable anti-Japan Korea."

From prior to WWII, Koreans were serving in the Japanese military. Prior to 1944, Koreans were not conscripted and only limited numbers of select volunteers were accepted. According to data of Japan's Ministry of Internal Affairs, during the period from 1938 to 1943, there were 1,300,880 Korean volunteers for the Japanese Army and 29,028 were accepted. In September, 1944, Conscription Law was enacted.

In November, 2000, an official of Japan's Ministry of Welfare and Labor reported the total numbers of Koreans serving in Japan's armed forces [during WWII period] were: Army - 143,211; Navy – 21,433; Navy Civilians - 73,348. Many Koreans were officers in the Japanese military, over half a dozen were generals. A Korean, Lt General Hong Sa-ik, commanded Japan's Southern Army's POW Command. He is an example of a Korean general in command of regular Japanese troops. How many countries had general officers from their colonies in command of soldiers of the occupying powers?

Another example of how Japan regarded Koreans is the death in the atomic bombing of Hiroshima of Prince Yi Wu, grandson of Emperor Gojong. Prince Yi was a Lt Col (promoted to Colonel posthumously) in the Japanese Imperial Army and stationed at Hiroshima. He was on his way to his duty station on horseback when the bomb fell. He died the next day in a hospital. His body was immediately flown back to Korea for a royal funeral. His aide, a Japanese officer, committed suicide after the funeral to atone for not protecting the prince. The bombing was on Aug 6, the funeral in Korea on Aug 15 attended by many Japanese dignitaries. August 15, 1945, is the date of Japan's surrender! That the Japanese placed such a high priority on this one individual amidst this horrendous chaos in Hiroshima and the pending doom of their empire demonstrates the degree of respect Japan had for a member of the Korean nobility. This is hardly the treatment that would be accorded a member of a brutalized slave colony.

As an annexed part of the Japan, the abduction of Korean women by the Japanese military as sex slaves is unthinkable. To say Korean men did nothing while their women were being abducted as sex slaves is an insult. There would have been a bloody uprising. Koreans are first class fighting men and hardly the type of people who would allow their women to be abducted and do nothing. There is not one recorded incident of resistance or a single witness to abduction by Japanese soldiers of Korean women.

Were Koreans helpless? Over a hundred thousand were serving in the Japanese military. There is even a story of a Korean kamikaze pilot. While the Japanese were dominant in the higher positions, most of the rank and file policemen were Koreans. The abduction of Korean women under those circumstances is unlikely. To most Koreans, however, the abduction of their women is believable because they believe an alternate history of Korea.

This issue has also affected our attitude toward those of Japanese ancestry in the U.S. In 2015, an article in a high school newsletter website in Southern California quoted a statement that Japanese Americans were involved in abduction of Korean women for Japan's comfort stations. The tone of the article supported the quoted statement. The school board defended the article as protected by freedom of speech. A libelous, racial, hate article against a minority group is protected as freedom of speech by a school board! Only after a Marine veteran of the Korean War brought in a lawyer was the article removed. In spite of its negative impact, California has also incorporated the teaching of unproven sex slave allegations against Japan in its school system.

Japanese explanations do not seem to have credibility and it is up to concerned Americans to explain the truth. This issue is not what it appears to be, it is like a malignant cancer and unless this anti-Japan campaign is recognized for what it is, it could have a very negative impact on the future of America and the free world.

B. SUMMARY OF CONTENTS

1. Comfort Stations. The Japanese military regulated brothels with the objective of minimizing rape and violence against the local populace and to curb venereal disease. Espionage and safety of troops were also of concern. Comfort stations were a place of rest and relaxation for troops and provided amenities other than prostitutes. Prostitutes were an adjunct to the comfort stations which provided various recreational services. Those proving prostitutes were referred to as special comfort stations and the prostitutes as comfort women.

2. Recruitment of Comfort Women.

There were a few cases in the Dutch East Indies of direct involvement by soldiers in the recruitment of prostitutes. These incidents involving involuntary women were punished as war crimes. These were exceptions. **A Dutch report clearly states the Japanese 16th Army which occupied much of the Dutch East Indies had regulations against use of involuntary women in comfort stations.**

There are Allied interrogation reports on recruitment of comfort women by comfort station operators and brokers. Japanese military records mention nothing about recruiting methods. One Japanese military regulation in Indonesia mentions operators being required to use local language in volunteer statements signed by comfort women. There was a Japanese Department of the Army directive warning against use of operators who use illegal recruiting practices.

Abduction of women and rape were punishable under Japanese military law. However, there were many instances of rape, notably during the early years of the war in China. Japanese records indicate this was of serious concern to the military.

There was only one U.S. war crime case involving involuntary prostitution. It involved a Japanese civilian in Guam. He was not connected with the Japanese military. **Australian records show only one case of rape by a military police officer. There were no reported cases involving involuntary comfort women.**

The documents show the majority of comfort women were Korean and Japanese. Chinese prostitutes are often mentioned. There are Japanese military regulations in this compilation on the use of authorized local brothels by troops in the Philippines, Burma, Indonesia, and China. **U.S. military interrogation reports of Korean comfort women and their operators indicate Korean women were recruited by civilian operators or their agents. The diary of a Korean comfort station operator also bears this out.** There records clearly identity comfort women as contract prostitutes.

3. Military Involvement in Comfort Station Operation. With few exceptions, **comfort station operators were non-military civilians**. Monthly reports by local Japanese consul generals in various Chinese cities identify comfort station operators with Korean comfort women as Korean. No Japanese operated comfort station was reported

with Korean women. The comfort stations were civilian operated businesses. This was also made clear in the diary of a Korean who ran a comfort station in Burma. Operating a comfort station was clearly a business.

4. Extent of military control. The word "regulated" has caused misunderstanding since it implies the direct control by the regulator. Comfort station regulations were conditions under which those doing business with the Japanese military, both operators and prostitutes, had to comply to conduct business. They gave special attention to the health of both the women and the soldiers and conduct of soldiers. In many cases, they specified the ratio to be used in sharing profits between operators and comfort women, usually with half of the women's earnings going to the operator.

5. Total number of comfort women.

The total number of comfort women could not be determined. Interrogation Report No. 49 mentions 702 comfort women being shipped to Burma in 1942. The estimated number of Japanese troops in Burma at time was 200,000. Recently, Lee Hong-hoon of Seoul National University estimated there at were, at most, 5,000 Korean comfort women. Professor Lee makes it clear they were not abducted. There is no evidence of large numbers of local women serving as comfort women.

One Japanese military order in North China, where comfort stations did not exist, stipulated that in its sector of responsibility, Chinese operated brothels would be allowed on the basis of one woman per assigned strength of 100 soldiers. In one interrogation report in SE Asia, the prisoner stated the number of comfort women in the area was one woman for 2,000 soldiers, and only available for officers.

6. Treatment of comfort women at the end of the war.

At war's end, Japan has been accused of abandoning and even executing the women. U.S. Interrogation reports of comfort women in Burma and the Philippines show Japanese troops evacuated the women with them when they could. Refer to the Burma Section of ATIS Report No. 120 and Report No. 163LD-1223 of this compilation.

On Timor [part of present-day Indonesia], Australian troops accepted the Japanese surrender. The comfort station was located in the city in a large building. The women had not been prisoners or mistreated by the Japanese military. The women were not interned by Australian troops but with the confinement of Japanese troops, there was a total lack of business. Japanese military script the women had accumulated had become worthless. The operator of the comfort house, a woman, made a request to the Australian commander and asked that Australian troops make use of the facility. The women were paid with "goodies" by the Australian until they (the women) were eventually sent home. None of the women were Indonesians. This information was obtained from a U.S. Army sergeant attached to Australian troops who served as the interpreter for the arrangement. He is a former California State Assemblyman and considered a credible source.

C. U.S./ALLIED MILITARY DOCUMENTS

     1. HQ, Island Command [U.S. Navy], Guam, [War Crimes] Serial No. 846, May 12, 1945.

     a. This was the charges/specifications in the war crimes trial of Samuel T. Shinohara, an inhabitant and resident of Guam. Among other charges (treason, assault and battery), he was found guilty of using duress on two local civilian females on Guam in Feb 42 to engage in prostitution. He was not in the Japanese military and not even a civilian employee of the military or government. He was an ethnic Japanese living in Guam. He was sentenced to hang, subsequently commuted to a prison sentence by U.S. Military Commission Order No. 11 [no date], U.S. Pacific Command and Pacific Fleet

     b. This case is mentioned because of it points out some significant facts:

     (1) The perpetrator was a resident civilian. The women were not physically coerced but their being pressured to serve as prostitutes was considered sufficient to justify the charge of war crimes.

     (3) **This case illustrates that the U.S. military did consider forcing a women into involuntary servitude as a prostitute was a war crime. And yet, there is not a single case on file in which U.S. authorities prosecuted any other Japanese civilian or soldier for forcing or using involuntary women as prostitutes on Guam or in any other area**.

     2. Summary of Prisoner of War Interrogation Report No. 49.

     a. This report is widely known for providing a detailed record of comfort women. It was prepared by the United States Office of War Information, Psychological Warfare Team, which was attached to U.S. Army Forces, India-Burma Theater. The prisoners were 20 Korean Comfort Girls. Date of Capture: August 10, 1944. Place Interrogated: Ledo Stockade. Date Interrogated: Aug 20 – Sept 10, 1944. Date of Report: October 1, 1944. Originally classified "Secret," declassified in 1973.

     b. The report provides an objective description of comfort women: how the women were recruited with advance loans, of signing contracts, of being paid, of not being under guard and free to go shopping, of being allowed to refuse customers, of joining officers in recreational activities and social dinners, of receiving gifts from soldiers and even of proposals of marriage and actual marriages. **There is no mention of abduction, rape, or brutality.** It throws a completely different light on the issue.

     c. The report mentions the girls **grossing fifteen hundred yen a month, then turning 50% to 60% to the "house master." According to a Yale University research, a female textile worker in Japan in 1939 earned less than 20 yen a month. In one year, a comfort woman would earn more than a life time in a textile factory.**

An advance loan of a few hundred yens was not a paltry sum at that time. A Japanese soldier's pay started at six yen a month.

        d. The report mentions the **operators were two Japanese civilians.** Their names and address are provided, obviously a husband and wife pair. While the names are Japanese names, their address is listed as present day Seoul, Korea, not Japan. At the time, many, if not most, Koreans used Japanese names and spoke fluent Japanese. **The ages of the Korean comfort women listed one teenager who was 19 years of age, four 20, with the rest over 21, eight being 25 or older.**

        e. Some direct quotes from the report follows:

"PREFACE:

        "This report is based on the information obtained from the interrogation of twenty Korean 'comfort girls' and two Japanese civilians captured around the tenth of August, 1944, in the mopping up operations after the fall of Myitkyina in Burma.

        "The report shows how the Japanese recruited these Korean 'comfort girls,' the conditions under which they lived and worked, their relations with and reaction to the Japanese soldier, and their understanding of the military situation.

        *"**A 'comfort women' is nothing more than a prostitute or professional camp follower attached to the Japanese Army for the benefits of the soldiers.** The word 'comfort girl' is peculiar to the Japanese. Other reports show the 'comfort girls' have been found wherever it was necessary for the Japanese Army to fight. This report however deals only with the Korean 'comfort girls' recruited by the Japanese and attached to their Army in Burma. The Japanese are reported to have shipped some 703 of these girls to Burma in 1942."*

"RECRUITING:

        *"Early in May of 1942 the Japanese agents arrived in Korea for purpose of enlisting Korean girls for 'comfort service' in newly conquered Japanese territories in Southeast Asia. The nature of this 'service' was not specified but it was assumed to be work connected with visiting the wounded in hospitals, rolling bandages, and generally making the soldiers happy. **The inducement used by these agents was plenty of money, an opportunity to pay off the family debts**, easy work, and the prospects of a new life in a new land – Singapore. On the basis of the false presentations many girls enlisted for overseas duty and were rewarded with an advance of a few hundred yens.* [For details on recruitment, refer to Report No. 120 on page 20 on interrogation of brothel owner].

        "The majority of the girls were ignorant and uneducated, although a few had been connected with the 'oldest profession on earth' before. The contract

*they signed bound them to Army regulations **and to work for 'house masters' for a period of from six months to a year depending on the family debt for which they were advanced money.***

"*Approximately 800 of thee girls were recruited in this manner and they landed with the Japanese 'house masters' at Rangoon around August 20th, 1942. They came in groups of eight to twenty-two. From here they were distributed to various parts of Burma, usually to a fair sized town near Japanese Army camps....*"

"*PERSONALITY:*

"*The interrogation shows **the average Korean 'comfort girl' to be about twenty five years old,** uneducated, childish, whimsical, and selfish. She is not pretty either by Japanese or Caucasian standards....*"

"*LIVING AND WORKING CONDITIONS:*

"*In Myitkyina, the girls were usually quartered in a large two-story house (usually a school building) with a separate room for each girl. There each girl lived, slept, and transacted business. In Myitkyina their food was prepared by and purchased from their 'house master' as they received no regular ration from the Japanese Army. **They lived in near-luxury** in Burma in comparison with other places. This was especially true of their second year in Burma. They lived well because their food and material was not heavily rationed and they had plenty of money with which to purchase desired articles. **They were able to buy cloth, shoes, cigarettes, and cosmetics to supplement the many gifts given them by soldiers who had received 'comfort bags' [a bag filled with miscellaneous goods from the home front]** from home.*

"***While in Burma they amused themselves by participating in sports events with both officers and men; and attended picnics, entertainments, and social dinners.** They had a phonograph; and in the town they were allowed to go shopping.*"

"*PRICE SYSTEM:*

"*The conditions under which they transacted business were regulated by the Army, and in congested areas regulations were strictly enforced. The Army found it necessary in congested areas to install a system of prices, priorities, and schedules for the various units operating in a particular area....*"

"*SCHEDULES:*

"*The soldiers often complained about congestion in the houses. On many occasions they were not served and had to leave as the army was very strict about overstaying leave. In order to overcome this problem the Army set aside certain days for certain units. Usually two men from the unit for the day were stationed at the house to identify the soldiers. A roving MP was also on hand to keep order. Following is the schedule used by....*

*"Soldiers would come to the house, pay the price and get tickets of cardboard about two inches square with price on the left side and the name of the house on the other side. Each soldier's identity or rank was then established after which he took his turn in line. **The girls were allowed the prerogative of refusing a customer.** This was often done if the person were too drunk."*

"PAY AND LIVING CONDITIONS:

"The 'house master' received fifty to sixty per cent of the girls' gross earning depending on how much of a debt each girl had incurred when she signed her contract. This meant that in an average month a girl would gross about fifteen hundred yen. She turned over seven hundred fifty to the 'master.' *Many 'masters' made life very difficult for the girls by charging them high prices for food and other articles.*

"In the latter part of 1943 the Army issued orders that certain girls who had paid their debt could return home. Some of the girls were thus allowed to return to Korea.

*"The interrogation further shows that the **health of these girls was good.** They were well supplied with all types of contraceptives, and often soldiers would bring their own which had been supplied by the army. They were well trained in looking after both themselves and customers in the matter of hygiene. A regular Japanese Army doctor visited the house once a week and any girl found diseased was given treatment, secluded, and eventually sent to a hospital. This same procedure was carried on within the ranks of the Army itself, but it is interesting to note that a soldier did not lose pay during the period he was confined."*

"REACTIONS TO JAPANESE SOLDIERS:"

This section only mentions the women's opinion about two Japanese commanders.

"SOLDIERS' REACTIONS:

*"The average Japanese soldier is embarrassed about being seen in a 'comfort house' according to one of the girls who said, 'When the place is packed he is apt to be ashamed if he has to wait in line for his turn.' However **there were numerous instances of proposals of marriage and in certain cases marriages actually took place.***

"All the girls agree that the worst officers and men who came to see them were those who were drunk and leaving for the front the following day. But all likewise agreed that even though very drunk the Japanese soldier never discussed military matters of secrets with them....

"The soldiers would often express how much they enjoyed receiving magazines, letters and newspapers from home. They also mentioned the receipt of 'comfort bags' filled with canned goods, magazines, soap, handkerchiefs, toothbrush, miniature doll, lipstick, and wooden clogs. The lipstick and clogs were definitely feminine and girls couldn't understand why the people at home were sending such articles. They speculated that the sender could only have had themselves or the 'native girls' in mind."

"REACTION TO THE MILITARY SITUATION:"

This section concerns the scant information the girls had of the military situation.

"It was the consensus among the girls that Allied bombings were intense and frightening and because of them they spent most of their last days in foxholes. One or two even carried on work there. The comfort houses were bombed and several of the girls were wounded and killed."

f. The final three sections of the report are *"RETREAT AND CAPTURE,"* *"PROPAGANDA,"* and *"REQUESTS."* An Appendix provides the names, ages, and addresses of the twenty women and the two operators. *"The retreat and capture of the 'comfort girls' is somewhat confused in their own mind."* This is covered in detail in this compilation in the Burma Section of Report No. 120 in the interrogation of the brothel owner. The owner's account provides more details and the only contradiction to that mentioned by the women is how much they knew of the nature of the work.

3. Summary of 163d Language Detachment Report No. 163 LD-1 0223.

a. The 163d Language Detachment was attached to Headquarters I Corps, U.S. Army, in the Philippines. Report No. 163LD-1 0223 is titled, "Combined Enemy Preliminary Report," and dated 21 May 1945. Classified Confidential, declassified 6/6/56.

b. This is an Interrogation Report of five comfort women captured by U.S. Forces in Luzon, Philippines in May, 1945. **Their ages are: 19, 22, 24, 28 and 28.** Two pairs are sisters. One is from Formosa (Taiwan). The other four are Korean.

c. Portions of interest are quoted in italics. Parts of special interest are highlighted in bold letters.

- *"Nationality : Korean.*
  Status   : Prostitutes in employ of Jap Army.

Place of Capture: Vic of Dingalan Bay, Tayabas Prov, Luzon.
Date of Capture: 19 May 45"

- *"**The families of all the women were extremely poor and in order to save their families the expense of caring for them, they were sold to a Geisha House in Korea.** They were sent to Taichu City, Formosa [present Taichung, Taiwan] and placed in the employ of the Army. They returned to Korea and on 29 Apr 44 left with 62 other women of both Jap and Korean nationality for the Philippines. They were still in the employ of the Jap Army. Upon arrival in the Philippines they were split up into small groups and sent to various army camps. 10 women, including subject EAs [enemy aliens], were sent to Higuchi L of C unit near Clark Field where they stayed at a Geisha House run by Mr. Taniguchi. From here they were sent to Sector Hq, Clark Field. Sometime in October 1944 they were sent to South San Fernando and joined Nakamura L of C Unit. 10 Jan 45, they withdrew from South San Fernando and enroute [sic] met up with Col Suzuki and his force. Col Suzuki told them that if they were captured they would be a disgrace to Japan [the Japanese military considered being taken POW as a disgrace] therefore they had better tag along with him. They went to Ipo. During the march Army personnel would go on ahead leaving two or three soldiers with the women. One woman died enroute [sic] and two others were left in Ipo because of illness. Late Jan 43, left Ipo and arrived Iloilo sometime in Apr 45. They saw many soldiers fall out and die from starvation enroute [sic]. About two weeks ago Col Suzuki took approx 300 able-bodied men and proceeded towards Umiray. They thought men were armed with rifles. Men headed up towards the mountains and not along the coast. Two of the women went with the group but the five EA decided to go off and fend for themselves. They followed the coastline northward. 18 May 44 they saw an LCM [landing craft medium] off the coast firing up into the hills above them. They waded out into the water and waved their arms and shouted. The crew of the LCM picked them up and took them to Dingalong Bay."*

4. Extract from report, "Military Intelligence Service, Captured Personnel & Material Branch, dated 24 April 1945. Date of interrogation 11 April, 1945," of three Korean civilian POWs.

a. This interrogation is a "Composite Report on Three Korean Navy Civilians List No. 78, dated 25 March 1945, Re "Special Questions on Koreans." The information sought was Korean attitudes about Japan.

b. **The questions asked about comfort women were: "Do Koreans generally know about the recruitment of Korean girls by the Japanese Army to serve as prostitutes? What is the attitude of the average Korean toward this program? Does the P/W know of any disturbance or friction which has grown out of this program?"** In the report, their response is provided on page 3, Item 18 of the report as follows:

*"**All Korean prostitutes** that PoW have seen in the Pacific **were volunteers or had been sold by their parents into prostitution.** This is proper in the Korean way of thinking but direct conscription of women by the Japanese would be an outrage that the old and young folks alike would not tolerate. **Men would rise up in a rage**, killing Japanese no matter what consequence they might suffer."*

5. Other Interrogation Reports.

    a. ATIS (Allied Translator/Interpreter Section) Interrogation Reports.

      (1) ATIS Interrogation Report No. 57, dated 17 Apr 43.

      Subject is Japanese soldier rescued from the sea off New Guinea coast by US Navy Patrol Boat. Subject stated: *"There were approximately 20 brothels in RABAUL, KOKOPO area and the remainder were in the town. Inmates were all Japanese women"*

      Subject made an interesting comment about attitude: *"He did not believe that natives of occupied territories should be treated as equals to the Japanese. **Owing to the Rescript of the Emperor MEIJI, natives, although not on the same footing as the Japanese, were not made slaves and were well treated."***

      (2) ATIS Interrogation Report No. 63, dated 19 Apr 43.

      Subject is a Japanese soldier, corporal, captured by Australian troops. PW had heard that: *"...there were brothels in RABAUL and believed they were run by civilians.... **The women in them were 'played out' Japanese."***

      (3) ATIS Interrogation Report No. 78, dated 15 May 43.

      Subject is a Japanese officer PW, 2/Lt, captured Trobriands, after his ship was sunk and he made it to shore. Subject ***"persisted in his statement that Japan was treating natives of occupied countries as equals...."***

      PW stated that he had heard there were Naval brothels in RABAUL staffed by **Japanese girls.** These were professionals from Japan.

      (4) ATIS Interrogation Report No. 94. dated 15 Jun 43.

      Subject is a medical captain, captured after making it to shore in New Guinea. In addition to reference to brothels, he comments on the attitude of the Japanese army towards locals.

."*PW believed the natives of occupied countries should be and were being treated as equals.* **PW insisted that the Army did not run brothels but merely supervised those run by civilians** *under an arrangement whereby supervision began with the war and ended immediately* after cessation of hostilities *In no case were natives enslaved or restricted in any way. He had not read the Rescript of MEIJI* [Emperor Meiji] *regarding treatment of prisoners of war and natives, but thought it was being followed."*

(5) ATIS Interrogation Report No. 104, dated 27 Jun 43.

Subject is a Japanese Army Sgt, captured in lifeboat, Trobriand. His statement on brothels: "*Although brothels were provided by the Army,* **there was only one woman to 2,000 troops,** *consequently only officers were accommodated.*"

(6) ATIS Interrogation Report No. 573, sated 23 Jan 45.

Subject is Japanese Army Air Force PFC, rescued from sea by US Navy near MOEMI. This is interesting in that unauthorized brothels operated by locals charged considerably more than authorized brothels.

Brothels in PI – Manila. **"Some were under Army jurisdiction. Others run by civilians were out of bounds**, *and MPs who tried to keep soldiers away frequented these places themselves. Girls at civilian houses were usually half caste Spanish-Filipinos and prices Yen 10-20.* **Those at Army controlled houses were Yen 2-3 with JAP and KOREAN girls.** *Despite the differences in prices civilian houses were more popular, as they were less crowded."*

b. Office of Strategic Services [OSS – forerunner of CIA] Reports.

(1) Office of Strategic Services, India-Burma Theater, New Delhi, 15 June 1945. Memo D-59, Subject: Interrogation on Moulmein, by OSS Det 404.

This is an interrogation report on a captain of the Indian National Army [fought on Japanese side] prisoner from Moulmein [Burma].

Questioned about the presence of Thai soldiers or civilians in Moulmein, his reply was:

"Source did not see any Thai soldiers or male civilians. He did see a few Thai girls in the bazaar one day. Somebody (name unknown) told him they were working with the Japanese (probably as comfort girls)."

Comment: Prisoner was not asked if the girls were being guarded by Japanese soldiers. It is obvious that the OSS did not consider "comfort women" as being abducted "sex slaves" or prisoners of the Japanese military.

(b) OSS Memorandum by Dr Schofield, undated, Subject: "Interrogation of Japanese Prisoners of War for Psychological Warfare." Extract follows:

"This summary is based on 10 interviews conducted by the writer with 12 Japanese prisoners between…February 8th and March 25th, 1944."

"While this groups represents a very small segment of Japanese fighting men in one small area of Burma, nevertheless the similarity of certain of their reactions may permit the deriving of a few conclusions valid for propaganda purposes in this theater."

Under the heading "Recreation" was the following: *"The system of 'comfort girl' was described. A contingent of these girls, mostly of Korean origin, is assigned to each regiment and made available to officers and men of each company one day in the week."*

Comment: Comfort Women is listed under "Recreation" and not some heading appropriate for abducted women being systematically raped. If Korean women were abducted sex slaves of the Japanese Army, the OSS would have used that fact to incite rebellion among the thousands of Koreans serving in the Imperial Japanese Army or incite an uprising in Korea. There are no records of any psychological warfare activity using comfort women as a theme. .

6. ATIS RESEARCH REPORT NO. 120 {Portions of this report are also covered in Section F – Japanese Military Documents}.

a. Report is titled, "Amenities in the Japanese Armed Forces," dated 15 November 1945. It provides information available to Allied authorities up to 31 March, 1945, on amenities furnished by the Japanese to their armed forces. The report covers the following: canteen stores; amusements; news; and mail. **Brothels are covered under "Amusements."**

"The Japanese insure one form of amusement by locating brothels in forward areas. One prisoner of war stated that brothels are immediately established where there are any large number of troops. ***Majority of the women in Japanese brothels are Japanese, Korean, and Chinese.*** *Although the Japanese apparently waste no time in establishing their brothels, it appears demand greatly exceeds the supply. This condition practically excludes the enlisted personnel, and only officers are able to take advantage of these places of business.*

*"There appears to be quite a bit of difference of opinion among prisoners of war as to who owns and controls the brothels. The statement of a prisoner of war, **who was a brothel owner in BURMA**, and several lists of brothel regulations which have been captured in South West PACIFIC Area, **indicate that brothels are privately owned but under military supervision. Information available indicates that the venereal (disease) rate among Japanese troops…is exceedingly low.***"

b. Brothels of Japan's Armed Force in Southeast Asia. Brothels regulations are quite detailed and only extracts are presented in this compilation.

(1) Burma. In the section on BURMA, the report provides an extract from an Interrogation Bulletin which covers the interrogation of the civilian brothel owner mentioned in Report No. 49, of 20 Korean comfort girls.

"Prisoner of War, his wife and sister-in-law had made some money as restaurant keepers in KEIJO [present day Seoul], KOREA, but their trade declining, they looked for an opportunity to make more money and applied to Army Headquarters in KEIJO for permission to take comfort girls from KOREA to BURMA…."

"Prisoner of war purchased 22 Korean girls, paying their families from 300 to 1000 yen according to the personality, looks and age of the girls. These girls were from 19 to 31. They became the sole property of prisoner of war and the Army made no profits from them…."

""Every 'comfort girl' was employed on the following contract conditions. She received fifty percent of her own gross takings and was provided with free passage, free food and medical treatment. The passage and medical treatment were provided by the Army authorities, the food was purchased by the brothel owner with the assistance of the Army supply depots. The owner made other profits by selling clothing, necessities and luxuries to the girls at exorbitant charges. When a girl is able to repay the sum of money paid to her family, plus interest, she should be provided with a free return passage to KOREA, and then considered free…."

Retreat and Capture.

*"Prisoner of war's group…arrived at MYITKYINA about Jan 1943. There were already two brothels established so altogether there were three brothels **with 63 girls**…."*

*"On 31 July [1944]. About midnight, **a party of 63 girls** from the three brothels…and brothel owners, etc., [Report No. 49 describes the "etc" as 'families and helpers] began their evacuation from MYITKYINA. They*

crossed the IRRAWADDY in ten small boats. The majority of the remaining troops had already departed...but the sick and wounded were left behind."

"The party then began to trek in the wake of retreating troops. On 7 August they became involved in a skirmish and in the confusion the party split up." The 20 Chinese girls remained behind in the jungle and gave themselves up to Chinese troops. *"One party of about 20 girls followed in the wake of the Japanese troops.... Prisoner of War's party took shelter in an abandoned native house where they remained for two days while prisoner of war tried to construct a raft."* With them was a wounded Japanese soldier. They were captured at the house on 10 August.

"Of the original party of 63 girls, four had died during the journey and two had been shot, mistaken for Japanese soldiers."

From this account, the following can be deduced:

- Comfort women were not being killed nor abandoned by retreating Japanese troops.

- There is no mention of any local women being among the comfort women at Myitkyina.

(2) Sumatra and Southwest Pacific. The report mentions brothels in SUMATRA and the Southwest PACIFIC Area. One brothel in SUMATRA is mentioned. It had two native women and six Chinese women.

(3) In Section V. CONCLUSIONS of the report, the following remarks are made about brothels:

*"The establishment of brothels under strict regulations is **sanctioned** by military authorities in any areas where there are large numbers of troops."* ["Sanctioned" does not mean the **military** "established" the brothels.]

7. U.S. National Archives Interagency Working Group's Final Report to U.S. Congress on War Crimes Records.

In April, 2007, the U.S. National Archives made a report to Congress of the results of its search for classified records still in the National Archives concerning war crimes during WWII. [The "Final Report of Nazi War Crimes and Japanese Imperial Government Interagency Working Group (IWG)," signed by Allen Weinstein, Archivist of the United States]. Salient paragraphs are presented below:

"Many people around the world had hoped that the IWG would unearth records that would help them document Japanese atrocities.

*"To these people, I state unequivocally that the IWG was diligent and thorough in its search for relevant records about war crimes in Asia. **The IWG uncovered and released few Asian Theatre records because few such U.S. records remain classified."***

Comments related to Japanese war crimes:

"The International Military Tribunal for the Far East (known as the Tokyo War Crimes Tribunal) began in May 1946. There were 28 Class A defendants..."

"Additional tribunals that sat outside of Tokyo judged over 5,500 individuals in more than 2,200 trials."

*"General MacArthur organized trials in Manila. Also, American Tribunals were held in Shanghai, the U.S. Navy held trials for crimes in the Pacific. **Once the trial records had served their administrative and legal purpose, they were transferred to the National Archives."***

To encourage the full review of records in the National Archives, the IWG published a research guide to assist in researching Japanese war crimes. [Edward Drea, et al., Researching Japanese War Crimes: Introductory Essay (Washington, DC), 2006]. Except for a few documents which remain classified, all classified material related to war crimes in the National Archives have been declassified and are available to the public. Entire report access: http://www.archives.gov/iwg/reports/final-report-2007.pdf.

D. DUTCH MILITARY REPORTS

1. General Comments. Dutch military reports consist mainly of Netherlands Forces Intelligence Service (NEFIS) Interrogation Reports. Many reports mention the topic of prostitution. Most of the interrogations are of Indonesians and much of the information is hearsay and not based on personal knowledge. Nevertheless, there are official records of a few cases where perpetrators of forced recruitment for prostitution were tried as war criminals. Many documents related to the trials are in Dutch and were not accessed; the documents in English and Japanese, however, were examined.

2. The Bart von Poelgeest Report.

The study by Dr. Poelgeest, then an officer of the Ministry of Interior of the Netherlands, was commissioned by the Dutch government in 1993. It is a comprehensive report on the recruitment, forced and voluntary, of European women for prostitution in the Dutch East Indies (present-day Indonesia) during the Japanese occupation in World War II. It also briefly touches upon recruitment of local women although that is not the focus of the study. **There was nothing in the report to indicate a policy or practice of mass abduction of women, European or locals, as comfort women**.

Some salient parts will be mentioned with proper attributions. Direct quotes from the report are in italics. Highlighted parts (in bold font) are done to show significant facts and are not highlighted in the original report.

. a. General Information.

"The study shows that during the Japanese occupation, the Japanese military forces or military authorities were responsible for procuring the services of prostitutes for Japanese soldier and civilians on the five large islands and a number of smaller islands of the Dutch East Indies. The women involved were not only of indigenous origin but also European Dutch and Indo-Dutch. The extent to which these women were forced into prostitution or provided their services voluntarily would only be established with any certainty if sufficient information were available on the general and specific circumstances in which they were recruited and on ensuing events."

"The study shows that in recruiting European women for their military brothels in the Dutch East Indies, the Japanese occupiers used force in some cases. *Of the two hundred to three hundred European women working in these brothels, 65 were most certainly forced into prostitution."*

"In the years prior to the Japanese occupation, the prostitutes in the Dutch East Indies were mainly of Indonesian or Chinese origin, although a number of European women were also involved, working either as madams of brothels or as prostitutes in brothels and elsewhere. According to the

*law applicable in the Dutch East Indies at the time, **the term European** referred not only to the 'totoks", or full-blooded Dutch, and other persons of European origin, such as Germans, Italians, Hungarians, Russians, Belgians, British etc., but also to persons of Eurasian and, since the Japanese Act of the early 1900s, **Japanese** origin living in the Dutch East Indies. **In addition to approximately seventy million Indonesians, there were thus approximately three hundred thousand Europeans living in the Dutch East Indies,** most of whom lived on the island of Java.*

*"...in Japan..., the practice of visiting brothels was not particularly frowned upon. The rules applicable in this regard to Japanese army and navy personnel were different from those applicable to Japanese civilians. **During the war in China in the 1930s, the occurrence of venereal disease among the troops had led to problems with deployment and the Japanese military forces therefore decided to set up military brothels as a preventive measure. In addition to local women, Japanese and Korean – Korea being part of the Japanese Empire – were recruited for the brothels in China.***

"...In January 1942, the first Japanese attack was launched on the Dutch East Indies and Borneo and Celebes were taken. The Japanese army landed on Java on 1 March 1942 and the Dutch East Indies capitulated a week later.

"...The territory of the Dutch East Indies was administered by the Japanese army and navy, the latter being responsible for the outlying islands, the former for Java and Sumatra. Java was administered by the 16th army, Sumatra by the 25th army. The supreme command was the 7th army at Singapore, which fell directly under the authority of the government in Tokyo, was responsible for these three districts of the former Dutch East Indies."

b. Japanese Military Policy Concerning Comfort Women...

"Neither the government in Tokyo nor the supreme command of the 7th army issued general regulations or instructions with regard to the establishment of military brothels in the former Dutch East Indies. There wee only a few general rules on the treatment of the local population and of prisoners of war and internees, but these did not include any regulations or exceptions relating to prostitution."

*"**In practice, it was the local military commanders who had to draw up regulations on the establishment of military brothels in their territory. The chief of staff of the 16th army on Java and thus head of the military administration there decided that a license was required for the establishment of a military brothel. A license was issued only if certain conditions were met**, relating to, for example, regular medical check-ups and payments. **A further precondition was that the women working in the brothels***

had to do so voluntarily: according to the regulations, a license would only be issued if the women involved signed a statement to the effect that they were providing their service voluntarily. Within the organization of the 16th army, the officer-in-charge of the commissariat (the 'heitan' officer) was responsible for issuing those licenses and for ensuring observance of the conditions under which they were issued. Such supervision was needed...as the women...frequently could not read the 'volunteer statement', which was written up in Japanese or Malay."

"The navy adopted a different approach on Borneo. In early September 1943, the Takeitai (the navy's military police comparable to the Kempeitai within the army) banned all relations between Japanese navy personnel and the local population, with the exception of the women working in the military brothels which were to be set up. The military government then instructed the federation of Japanese companies on the island to set up and supervise these brothels, but military authorities later assumed control."

"**Apart from women of Japanese and Korean origin, the women recruited for the Japanese military brothels in the Dutch East Indies came from three groups, i.e. Indonesian women, European women living in the internment camps, and European women living outside the camps**."

"More than 150,000 Europeans were interned either as prisoners of war or civilian internees, with approximately 220,000 of their number...stayed out of the camps. "

c. Java.

"First stage (mid-1942 to mid-1943)"

"**There are no cases on record of women being forcibly taken from the internment camps to work in brothels in the period between mid-1942 and mid-1943.**"

"Second Stage (mid-1943 to mid-1944)"

"In the period between mid-1943 and mid-1944, the use of direct physical force by the army and the Kenpeitai to recruit women for brothels became more prominent feature of Japanese policy...."

"**In the last week of April 1944, the brothels in which European women had been put to work were suddenly shut down after a colonel of the Ministry of War in Tokyo, who was responsible for supervising both the civilian and prisoner-of-war camps, had made a tour of inspection of the internment camps on Java.**"

"The colonel informed Batavia, Singapore and Tokyo of his findings and recommended the immediate closure of the Semarang brothels. The headquarters at Batavia responded immediately by sending orders to this effect to the general responsible in Semarang. After the war, this general, a number of his staff members and other soldiers, the Japanese pimps and the doctor responsible for conducting the examinations, were tried before the temporary war tribunal at Batavia."

"Third stage (mid-1944 to mid-1945)"

"After the (temporary) closure of a number of military brothels in which European women worked in May 1944, including those at..., probably as a result of the evaluation of the Tokyo inspector's report..., a number of privately-run brothels , including those at..., were shut down too."

d. *"Conclusion.*

From the evidence contained in the documents, it may be concluded that military brothels were established on all the large islands of the Dutch East Indies during the Japanese occupation and that European women were put to work in those establishments on.... Though their number cannot be determined exactly on the basis...of the material available, some two hundred to three hundred European women were probably involved, most of whom on the island of Java."

"To conclude, the documents available reveal of the two hundred to three hundred European women working in the Japanese military brothels in the Dutch East Indies, some sixty-five were most certainly forced into prostitution."

3. Comfort Women Dutch War Crimes Cases.

a. The Semarang Incident.

The Semarang Incident refers to the war crimes case involving the involuntary recruitment of Dutch women for a comfort station in the Dutch East Indies. It is among the most well known instance of involuntary recruitment of women. Semarang is a city on the island of Java in present day Indonesia. Original reports are mostly in Dutch. The Poelgeest Report provides some details. The following is a brief summary of that case derived from the Poelgeest Report, Japanese documents and secondary sources. As more research is conducted there may be slight variances.

In October, 1943, due to the worsening military situation, the internment camp at Surabaja was closed and inmates moved to other camps. In late February 1944, some Japanese soldiers appeared at Camp #4, which was guarded by local native police, and removed six Dutch women, reportedly for clerical work. This happened also at other camps. Some 35 women in all were selected, made to sign documents agreeing to become prostitutes, and placed in comfort stations. A few of the women were volunteers, others not. The following month, at the end of March, 1944, Camp #4 came under the direct military jurisdiction of the Japanese Army.

The Japanese military camp commander was informed by inmates that some women had been taken away. He said he would look into it and did nothing. A month later, in late April, 1944, Major Odamura from Japanese Army Headquarters in Tokyo arrived to inspect the camp and learned from inmates that some women had been taken away to comfort stations. After looking into the matter, he advised Headquarters Southern Army in Singapore and Japanese Army Headquarters in Tokyo to close the brothels. On May 10, the women were released. After the war, all involved were charged with war crimes and tried by Dutch authorities.

The Japanese officer held responsible was Major Okada, who had taken this action to accommodate visiting military cadets because he was concerned with venereal disease among local prostitutes. He had cleared this with Headquarters16th Army. Authorization from Headquarters 16th Army specified that the women voluntarily leave the detention camp and voluntarily (free will) agree to work in a comfort station knowing it would be for prostitution.

Although Major Okada claimed he had left the recruiting to others, he and 13 individuals were tried for war crimes by Dutch authorities. Twelve were convicted. Major Okada was sentenced to death. Others received sentences confining them from 2 to 20 years. [Major Okada's verdict can be found in Japanese at wam-peace/ianfu-kokubunsho/list/m-all-list.html. Document #264]

While the Poelgeest Report mentions some 65 Dutch women being forced into prostitution, further research is needed to confirm other war crimes trials involving Dutch women other than the Semarang case.

b. Forced Prostitution: Six Daughters of Insurgents, East Indies.

This case was tried by the war crimes court. The incident is covered in War Crimes Evidentiary Document Nr. 5591, dated June 7, 1946. It involved six daughters of 40 locals who were captured after an attack on the Japanese military. Six of the daughters of the insurgents were raped and forced into a comfort house for approximately eight months by the local Japanese commander, a lieutenant. This was not a case of recruitment of comfort women, this was clearly abduction and rape, a war crime, and it was tried as such.

c. Forced Prostitution: Women Suspected of Having Relationships with Japanese Soldiers, West Borneo.

This case was tried as a war crime. The following is from Evidentiary Document No. 1330, prepared by Capt J. N. Heybruck, Dutch Intelligence Officer, July 5, 1946. A Japanese naval commander of a security detachment at Ponchanak (sic), West Borneo, in early 1943, issued orders that Japanese were not to enter into close relationship with Indonesian or Chinese women. A number of women were falsely accused of having a relationship with Japanese military men and involuntarily made to serve as comfort women. The women received 2/3 of their earnings, 1/3 was used for food and other expenses.

4. Dutch Interrogation Reports. There are many Netherlands Forces Intelligence Reports. Only those cases involving comfort women are included. **None of the reports are based on direct interrogation of the women involved or operators of comfort stations**.

NEFIS Interrogation Reports on Prostitution. These reports are of interest in that **there is no concrete evidence of abductions of local women for use as sex slaves.**

(1) NEFIS Report, dated 27 Dec 44, "Compilation of NEFIS Interrogation Report Nos. 450, 538, 553, 555, 580, 563, 585, 589 and 593."

"..., *location of brothels in Batavia (West Java): Gang Chaulan housed only Japanese women. Behind ...in houses on ...European and Javanese women were seen. Informant is unable to say whether or not the women were forced into prostitution....*"

Comment: From the questioning, it appears interrogators were searching for evidence of involuntary recruitment.

(2) NEFIS Report, dated 6 Dec 44, "Compilation of NEFIS Interrogation Reports Nos. 534, 552, 567, 568, 579, 586, 587, 588, and 592.

- "*XIII. General. <u>Prostitution</u>: A brothel was located in... having as inmates a very large number of Indonesian girls and women, for the exclusive use of Japanese military personnel. **They were carefully selected from what would appear to be a number of willing applicants**. No girl or woman who had given birth of a child was eligible. Those selected received a premium of 300 guilders and an outfit of fine clothing of a desirable type. The procurer informed him (informant) there was a fairly high turn over of inmates at the brothel, as immediately a girl developed VD she was summarily discharged and replaced.*"

(3) NEFIS Report, dated 6 Nov 44, Compilation of NEFIS Interrogation Report Nos. 455-469.

- "*An informant who was in Malang (East Java) in Nov 43,*

states that many Eurasians, Menadonese and Javanese women from 17 to 30 years of age were taken from their homes and, after being medically examined, installed in brothels located in the Hotel ... and in European houses in .... Others were forced to work in restaurants. Those unfit to or unable to carry on were returned to the original internment camp or allowed to go home."

(4) NEFIS Report, dated 29 Oct 44, Compilation of NEFIS Interrogation Report Nos. 366-378, 404-407, and 410-417.

Interrogation of Indonesians. Prostitution: *"During '43 at Solo (Mid-Java) - A Javanese* [native of Java] *who lived in Mid-Java selected girls for prostitution for use by Japanese troops. During '43, at Solo (mid-Java) a Chinese was given a permit to use the Russche Hotel for prostitutes for Japanese officers. He selected girls from the village with the help of the assistant village chief offering them work for money. One informant from Amboebe (E Java) said village girls were selected for restaurants and for prostitution."*

(5) NEFIS Report, dated 6 Nov 44, compilation of Interrogation Report Nos. 455-469.

Interrogation of Indonesians. Prostitution. *"Informant who was in E Java stated that in '43, many Eurasian, Menadonese and Javanese women from 17 to 30 from villages and internment camps were utilized as prostitutes in hotels and European houses in Samaanweg. Others worked in restaurants."*

(6) NEFIS Report, dated 29 Dec 44, Compilation of Interrogation Report Nos. 450, 538, 553, 555, 580, 583, 585, 589-593.

Interrogation of Indonesians. Prostitution. Brothels at Octavia (W Java). Gang Chaulan housed only Japanese women. Eurasian and Javanese women were seen at another brothel. Informant could not say whether women were forced into prostitution.

(7) NEFIS Report, dated 10 Jan 45, Compilation of Report Nos. 818, 820-888.

Interrogation of Indonesians. Soerebaja (E Java). July 44. Informant stated most prostitutes were Javanese. Some Japanese women were seen.

(8) NEFIS Report, dated 27 Jun 45, Compilation of Interrogation Report Nos. 886. 887 and 888.

Interrogation of Indonesians. E Java. In Jul 44, informant

saw five European women in a hotel on the Abon-abon. One of the hotel servants told informant the women were prostitutes for Japanese officers.

(9) NEFIS Report, dated 7 Feb 45, Compilation of Interrogation Nos. 997-1005.

Interrogation of Indonesians. Wasale Bay. One informant stated that in Jun 44 he had seen 100 Javanese, 90 Chinese, 30 Menonese and 30 Japanese women engaged in prostitution.

(10) NEFIS Interrogation Report No. 1244, dated 9 Mar 45.

Interrogation of Indonesian. Halmahera. Informant saw a number of Indonesian women quartered in a building. They were controlled by a Chinese woman.

(11) NEFIS Report, dated 5 May 45, compilation of Interrogation Report Nos. 1590-1630.

Interrogation of Indonesian. Prostitution. Ternate Island, Nov 44. Informant states shortly after occupation of Ternate Island, the Japanese installed a collection and distribution center for young women for the purpose of prostitution. Two large brothels were organized and women of various races.... Only single women were eligible.

(12) NEFIS Interrogation Report No. 751, dated 31 Dec 44.

Interrogation of Indonesian. Prostitution: Informant heard that 50 Japanese women were brought by ship from E Java for use of Japanese Navy personnel only.

(13) NEFIS Report, dated 23 Mar 45, Compilation of Reports Nos. 1235-1238.

Interrogation of Indonesian. Prostitution, Tarakan, NE Borneo. *"About 50 Japanese women were housed near a hospital at 'Ladang."*

(14) NEFIS Interrogation Report No. 1252, dated 10 May 45.

Interrogation of Indonesian school teacher. Prostitution in N. Celebes. There were two houses in Prost, one for officer with 30 women, one for NCO/men with 50 women. Women were from various locales. **They received monthly salaries, kept all the money given by clients.** Clothing, etc, were provided. The women had to pass physical exams, a regular check by a physician. In event of disease, treated at hospital then sent home. They were at liberty to leave the brothels for fixed periods.

(15) NEFIS Report, dated 12 Feb 45, Compilation of Reports Nos. 1066, 1196-1253.

Interrogation of Indonesian. Ambon Island. Brothel. Women were locals and Eurasian women. Women appeared normal and showed no sign of distress.

(16) NEFIS Interrogation Report No. 422, dated 23 Oct 43.

Interrogation of Indonesian. Sumatra. At Medan, officers have access to Japanese women brought from Japan. Others have access to Indonesian women.

5. Comments on Indonesia.

Indonesia has the fourth largest population in the world and is the largest country in Asia after China and India. It consists of approximately 20,000 islands spanning 3,000 miles. During the Japanese occupation, different parts were under the control of the 25th Army, the 16th Army, and the Japanese Navy.

The Japanese military was involved in teaching self-government and training the Indonesian military, not plundering and raping the country. At the end of the war, Indonesians opposed the return of the Dutch. Many Japanese soldiers remained in Indonesia and fought for Indonesian independence against Dutch forces following the end of WWII. One Japanese source mentions 3,000 remaining, with 1,000 dying in the battle for Indonesian independence, 1,000 returning to Japan after the war, and 1,000 who chose to remain in Indonesia after independence. Those who died in the fighting are interred at the Kalibata Heroes Cemetery in South Java.

The Semarang case clarifies two main points, that official Japanese military policy did not condone the use of involuntary women as comfort women and that, in spite of official policy and regulations, violations did take place. In the case of the Dutch women at Semarang, when an inspector from Tokyo learned of their situation, they were immediately released. A cursory inspection of comfort stations would not have revealed their involuntary status since, reportedly, the women had all signed statements saying they were voluntarily serving as comfort women. Also, the women were being paid. These facts are not in the official documents but were obtained from secondary sources. There are no reported cases of mass abductions, rapes and violence against locals by soldiers with the exception of harsh punishments of locals for looting.

Less than half a dozen cases of war crimes trials involving use of local women as prostitutes were found. The estimated total number of involuntary local women was at most a few hundred. Had abduction and forced prostitution been widely practiced, considering the population and size of Indonesia, the number of incidents would be considerably higher.

E. AUSTRALIAN WARTIME RECORDS

1. Australian War Crimes Trials.

After WWI, the northwestern part of New Guinea which had been controlled by Germany came under Australian mandate. At the end of WWII, according to a study by D.C.S. Sissons, "The Australian War Crimes Trial and Independence, 1942-51," Australia tried 924 Japanese soldiers for suspected war crimes, 644 were convicted, and 148 executed. Victims of Japanese atrocities, in addition to Australian POWs, included natives, local Chinese and Caucasians. The area covered Borneo, Sarawak, Ocean Islands, Nauru, and New Britain. The war crimes trials involved Australian POWs in Burma, Siam, and Hainan. There were 12 trials involving natives, 2 local Chinese, and 5 local Caucasians. **None involved local women being abducted or forced into serving as comfort women.**

There was one trial for rape. A Japanese military police sergeant used physical coercion and threats to get a Chinese woman to consent to sexual intercourse. He was convicted by the war crimes court and sentenced to death. He did not exercise his right to submit a petition to the conforming authority to seek mitigation of the sentence. According to the Japanese defending officer, General Imamura, the Commander-in-Chief of Japanese Forces in the area, regarded rape by a military policeman such a heinous crime that he had forbidden the condemned to submit an appeal in this case.

2. Gordon Thomas, a former editor of "The Rabaul Times," spent three years in Rabaul while it was under Japanese occupation. He mentions Japanese and Korean comfort women arriving soon after Japanese troops occupied Rabaul. Thomas estimates 3,000 comfort women in Rabaul. The U.S. Strategic Bombing Survey gives an estimate of 500 to 600. Thomas mentions comfort women visiting the ice house where he worked to get ice. The women were not under guard. According to Thomas, comfort women were being sent home in 1943 and all of them were gone by the end of that year.

F. JAPANESE GOVERNMENT/MILITARY DOCUMENTS

1. RESEARCH REPORT NO. 120, dated 15 November 1945, contains a number of translated Japanese military regulations on brothels. The research report was by ATIS (Allied Translator and Interpreter Section), Supreme Commander of the Allied Powers. Some parts of interest were covered under Allied Reports. Other points of interest are mentioned here.

a. Manila. Extract from a translation of a bound booklet titled, "Rules for Restaurants and Houses of Prostitution," issued in Feb 43, by Lt Col Onishi, Manila Direct Lines Squad.

(1) Under General Regulations:

- Para 3: *"If and when various managers meet with difficulties, the officer in charge of Manila sector may either close the business or temporarily suspend it. In each case, they will present a statement for recompense for any losses or for any other inconveniences."*

(2) Under Part 2, Business Operations:

(a) Para 6: ***"Persons receiving permission to open business*** *will thereupon determine the number of personnel needed, and will submit three copies of their personnel list...,* ***one copy of the personal histories of employees,..."***

(b) Para 7: *"Managers intending to change the personnel of their establishment must secure the permission of.... Hostesses, geishas and waitresses wishing to leave the establishment must submit a request....* ***When the hostesses, geisha and waitresses are to be replaced, a request for permission to do so must be submitted...."***

(c) Para 8: *"Managers intending to increase the number of hostesses, geisha and waitresses, maids and others will so inform....* ***Permission is necessary before anyone joins the establishment."***

(d) Para 9: *"...managers who cannot maintain discipline will be removed."*

(e) Para 10: ***"Hostesses, geishas, waitresses, maids may, as a general rule, may be rehired at the expiration of their contract."*** *"Those wishing to continue their employment will so notify...."* *When the medical authorities consider it suitable to discontinue the services of anyone for reasons of health, they will notify....* ***The latter will facilitate the return home of such persons."***

(f) Para 16: *"**Half of the income of hostesses will be allocated to the managers.**"*

(g) Para 19: *"Expenses of food, light, charcoal and bedding for hostesses (geishas and waitresses) will be the responsibility of the managers."*

(h) Para 21: *"As far as possible, managers will encourage hostesses (geishas and waitresses) to save money."*

(i) Para 30: *"Hostesses (prostitutes and waitresses)...are forbidden to have intercourse beyond the premise of the house of relaxation. They must have the permission of ...**to attend parties for soldiers** and civilians."*

(j) Para 34: *"Entry to or permission to use the facilities of the house of relaxation may be refused to the following persons:*

> *a. Intoxicated person.*
> *b. Persons carrying liquor.*
> *c. Persons who may exert bad influence."*

(3) Under Part Six – Regulations for Special Clubs.

- Para 11. *"The officer in charge of Manila Sector for Communication Duties, will, as a general rule, **not permit the employment of minors as geisha or waitresses.** In certain circumstances, however, minors may be employed as maids."*

b. Manila Air Depot. Translation of bound mimeographed and hand-written regulations on the use of its brothel. Dates of all files are from Aug 44 to Oct 44. The file on brothel regulation contains the following:

(1) Para 4b: *"**There must be no act of violence or drunkenness, nor any unreasonable demands made of the house employees.**"*

(2) Para 5: *"Anyone violating the above rule will thereafter be denied entrance to the house."*

c. Shanghai Sector. Translation of ATIS Report #120 on regulations governing special brothels in the Shanghai sector.

(1) Under regulations governing the use of brothels, are the following:

(a). Para 2. *"**Those who commit violence..., those who annoy others and are dangerous, are strictly forbidden to use this brothel.**"*

(b) Para 11. ***"The prostitutes will posses licenses...."*** The license has the name of the prostitute, brothel, and has a statement signed by the Japanese Sector Commander and states: *"This is to verify the above person is permitted to conduct business."*

(c) Para 14: ***"Unlicensed prostitutes are strictly prohibited from plying their trade."***

(2) Under regulations governing the operation of special brothel are the following:

(a) Para 2: ***"If a person working in a brothel conducts herself improperly or acts in a manner contrary to regulations, she will be suspended or dismissed from the business***.*"*

(b) Para 8: *"The prostitute and the operator will share equally the proceeds of the work done by the prostitute."*

d. Tacloban. Translation of bound mimeographed file titled, "Tacloban Brothel Regulations, undated, issued by Matsunaga Force.

(1) In the regulations setting provisions for the operation of brothels is the following:

(a) Para 2: **"Places called brothels in these regulations are special brothels operated with Filipino women (licensed prostitutes)."**

(2) Under rules for those making use of brothels are the following.

(a) Para 7b: *"Those who are under the influence of liquor and those who are disorderly are prohibited from entering the brothels."*

(b) Para 7d: ***"There will not be any act of violence or coercion either against the women in the brothels or against operators of the brothels."***

(c) Para 7e: *"Payment will be made in advance in war notes."*

e. Baruen. Translation of bound, handwritten, mimeographed document titled, "Brothel Regulations," dated Aug 44.

- Para 7: *"Those making use of the brothel must strictly obey the following provisions.*

    (a) "Maintaining their generosity as military men and heeding the preservation of military secrets.

    (b) "They must not make demands on those working in the brothel other than as regulated, and must not be drunk or disorderly."

  f. Rabaul. Translation of miscellaneous items concerning naval brothel in Rabaul, undated. Naval brothels are referred to as "Special Warehouses" in the report.

    (1) Para 6: ***"Hostesses will refuse pleasure to** those who...."*

    (2) Para 8a: *"The uniform of petty officers and sailors when entering and leaving the special warehouses will be dress uniform"*

    (3) Para 9: *"Violation of any of the above regulations by the hostess will result in the **withdrawal of their right to practice**."*

2. Japanese Foreign Ministry Documents.

  a. Japanese Consul General Reports on Status of Countrymen and Businesses in Chinese Cities. [Details on other businesses omitted by author]

    (1) Jiujiang, Central China. Consulate Report No. 561, 11/8/38.

Japanese Operated Businesses:

Special Comfort Station	15
Japanese Operators	42 men, 25 women, 1 child
Japanese Comfort Women	107
Total Japanese Businesses	84
Total Japanese	357

Korean Operated Businesses:

Special Comfort Station	9
Korean Operators	26 men, 8 women, 3 children
Korean Comfort Women	143
Total Korean Businesses	17
Total Koreans	198

    (2) Nanchang, Central China. Consulate Report No. 217, dated August 9, 1939.

Japanese Operated Businesses:

Japanese Comfort Station	3
Japanese Operators	5 men, 3 women
Japanese Comfort Women	8
Total Japanese Businesses	84
Total Japanese	224

Korean Operated Businesses:

Korean Comfort Station	8
Korean Operators	19 men, 9 women
Korean Comfort Women	94
Korean Operated Businesses	31
Total Korean	200

       (3) Chiaohu, Central China. Consulate Report No. 170, dated August 2, 1939.

Japanese Operated Businesses:

Japanese Comfort Stations	4
Japanese Operators and	
Japanese Comfort Women	10 M, 31 W, 2 children
Total Japanese Businesses	382
Total Japanese	685

Korean Operated Businesses:

Korean Comfort Station	2
Korean Operators/comfort women	2 men, 30 women, 1 child
Total Korean Businesses	39
Total Koreans (Incl comfort women)	96

       (4) Report by Governor General of Taiwan on situation in Guangdong, Report No. 37, March 15, 1942.

Total Countrymen (Mainland Japanese, Taiwanese, Korean)

Total Type of Business:	94
Total number of Businesses:	1,044
Total Comfort Stations:	44
Total Japanese	5,468 men, 3,889 women
Total Taiwanese	185 men, 399 women
Total Koreans	2,715 men, 444 women

[Numbers employed in comfort stations not listed]

b. Comments on Foreign Affairs Department Documents.

(1) The reports are on the status of Japanese countrymen in Chinese cities. Countrymen are listed as Japanese, Koreans and Taiwanese. No others are listed. This means the Japanese regarded Koreans and Taiwanese, not as foreigners, but as countrymen. **These reports provide concrete evidence many comfort stations were operated by Koreans, a fact not widely known outside Korea and Japan.**

(2) Koreans were engaged in a myriad of businesses in addition to operating special comfort stations. These comfort stations are not listed separately or otherwise annotated to indicate they were anything special or other than just another one of the businesses. **They were not operated by the military or by military employees.** Prostitution was legal and operating a brothel was not considered an illegal activity. Types of business operated by Koreans, in addition to comfort stations, include the following: photo shops, retail stores, restaurants, tofu shops, doctors, transportation business, trading companies, watch shops, medicine stores, barbers, and hotels.

(3) **Korean operators of special comfort stations in many cases had women and children, in other words, families. This is evidence that they were not single men who were part of the Japanese Army. The same applied to Japanese operated comfort stations.**

(4) In all reports, special comfort stations operated by Japanese had Japanese comfort women, and those operated by Koreans had Korean comfort women. **There is not a single report that lists any Korean comfort women in a Japanese operated comfort station.** There were many reports on the same city at different times but showed no significant changes.

3. Other Japanese Military Documents

a. Department of the Army Directive to Northern China Area Army and Central China Area Army Warning of Illegal Recruitment Practices, dated March 4, 1938.

The report is a directive warning military commands that there are recruiters who smear the dignity of the military. It directs the military and police to be on the lookout for anything that looks like abduction. This report has been cited by some historians as concrete evidence of military involvement in the recruitment of comfort women.

While that may be the case, it does not clarify whether the military was actually involved in recruiting. While the military authorized comfort women and operators to do business in their sector, it did not mean the military was involved in the actual recruiting. Nowhere is there any evidence of guidance or directives to the military on procedures or type of contracts to be used in the recruitment of comfort women.

In view of the meticulous details of comfort station operations which the Japanese put in writing, if recruitment of comfort women was by the government or the military, it would be logical for detailed recruiting procedures and sample contract forms, amounts of money allowed to be paid in advance, etc, to exist. Nothing of that sort has been found.

b. Department of the Army Directive No. 1955, dated Sep 14, 1941, concerning Incidents in the China Theater and the Necessity for Education and Guidance of Troops. This report covers lessons learned and the need to preserve military discipline.

There is nothing specific about the recruitment of women for comfort stations. The Directive is lengthy and stresses the importance of educating the troops and minimizing incidents. Some excerpts follow:

- *"Special Characteristics of Crimes and Misbehavior in China.*

"With increase of troops and in contrast to many distinguished acts of valor, there have been many acts of looting, rape, arson and killing of prisoners, acts which are contrary to the true nature of our Imperial Army and make difficult our task of establishing permanent peace in the Far East, and makes common citizens our enemies... This fact must be pounded into every last soldier.... Special attention must be paid to conduct of soldiers immediately after a battle when troops are worked up.... The ignorance of military laws concerning misconduct...we must avoid ending up having to punish a soldier who has been decorated for valor because he was ignorant of the law...."

- There is mention of the special attention that must be paid on the conduct of soldiers, the necessity for educating troops before battle concerning military laws against misconduct, and the special efforts that must be made to provide amenities and the benefits of providing brothels with comfort women as a preventive to troops taking vengeance against the local population.

[Penal Code of the Imperial Army, enacted April 9, 1908.

Part 9. Looting and Rape.

Article 86. On the battlefield or territory occupied by the Imperial Army, anyone looting of property of local populace will be punished by imprisonment of over one year. In the process of the foregoing, anyone who rapes a woman/girl will be punished by indefinite prison term of seven years or more.

Article 88. In the performance of crimes of foregoing two Articles, anyone who causes injury to victim will be punished by indefinite imprisonment of over seven years. In event of causing death of victim, penalty will be death or indefinite imprisonment.

Article 88, Part 2. In the war zone or territory occupied by the Imperial Army, anyone committing rape of woman/girl will be subject to indefinite imprisonment or imprisonment of one or more years, If injury is caused to victim, penalty will be indefinite imprisonment of prison term of over 3 years. In event of death of victim, penalty will be death, indefinite imprisonment, or prison term of 7 years or more.]

c. Northern China Area Army Headquarter Directive, dated July 14, 1938, titled, "Strict enforcement of soldiers' compliance with regulations concerning conduct towards inhabitants." The Directive mentions lack of sufficient troops and the presence of communist guerilla activity were the main reason for difficulty in pacification efforts but unlawful conduct of soldiers toward local people was having a severe negative impact. Rape was especially damaging. **The directive ordered commanders to pay special attention to rape prevention.** It mentioned rape is not only a criminal act in itself but it interferes with military operations and thus is also an act of treason. Any commander who disagrees is unpatriotic. It stressed the need to eliminate resistance by strictly controlling individual soldiers and to arrange for comfort stations.

d. NORTH CHINA. 3d Mountain Artillery Regiment Regulation commanded by Colonel Takamori, dated October 11, 1940.

The portion concerning **rules for comfort station operated by Chinese operators with Chinese women** is translated below in italics. The comment on the number of women being on a ratio of 1 for 100 soldiers is interesting.

Regulations concerning business operations by Chinese comfort station operators within our area of responsibility. The purpose is to moderate the killer instinct of soldiers and maintain military order and discipline....

For locals to qualify, the following must be met:

1. *Proper identification, travel authorization....*
2. *Must be a registered resident.*
3. ***Number of women will be on a ratio of 1 for 100 soldiers.***
4. *Employees must have proper identification.*
5. ***All employees must submit resumes.***
6. *All employees will have health inspection once a month, comfort women once every 10 days.*
7. *Report revenue for month.*

41

Rules for soldiers:

1. *Permits will be used.*
2. *Turn over money and permit to comfort station.*
3. *No food or drinks allowed.*
4. ***No act of violence against operator or women.***
5. *No borrowing or lending of money to operator or women.*
6. *Time of use.* [This is broken down by rank. Also rate. No tips.]

----

e. North China. Independent Siege Heavy Artillery, 2d Battalion Internal Regulations, dated Mar 16, 1938. Major Mamba commanding. Section related to use of comfort station is presented. There is no data on whether one operator had comfort women of different nationalities or whether the price structure was meant to apply to the different (Japanese, Korean or Chinese) comfort stations. Price differences most likely result from language ability of the women and not physical attributes.

- Different days of the week are designated for different units.

- *Time is limited to one hour per person. Rate as follows:*
  Chinese 1 yen   Korean 1 yen 50 sen   Japanese 2 yen
  Charge for officers and warrant officers will be twice that listed.

- *Caution:*
  - *No drinking in the facility.*
  - *Strict compliance with time limit and payment.*
  - ***No violence against operators.***

- *Operators.*
  - *Must not service Chinese men.*
  - *Must not provide drinks.*
  - *Must not do business elsewhere.*
  - *Must possess health permit.*

f. North China. Japanese 14th Division, Medical Company Journal for November 1938. The part related to Charge for Alcoholic Beverages and Prostitutes is interesting. **Negotiating with local merchants for prices is not an expected conduct of an Army accused of raping and looting across Asia.** Of note is that the negotiated rate for a Chinese prostitute in town is comparable with that of a comfort station.

"The following was decided after meeting with operators of local drinking and brothels:

> - *Sake*   *One "go"*   *50 sen*
> [A "go" is 1/10 of a large (1.8 liter) sake bottle]
> - *Beer*   *One bottle*   *80 sen*
> - *Prostitutes*   *One hour*   *Soldier*   *2 yen*
>   *NCO*   *3 yen*
>   *Above Warrant Officer 4 yen*

> **- *Sale of alcoholic beverages in establishment providing prostitutes is strictly prohibited.***"

      g. China. "Regulations Concerning Operation of Special Comfort Stations" of Morikawa Unit (Regiment), dated Nov 13, 1939.

      The regulation applied to the area of responsibility of the regiment, reason for authorizing special comfort stations, and the two towns in which they are to be authorized. Parts of the regulation of interest follows:

      Paragraph 7. ***"All expenses needed for the special comfort station will be borne by the operator."*** This clearly established that comfort stations were not operated by nor funded by the military.

      Subparagraphs stipulate authorized users, hours of operation, requirement for posting price, collecting of price and "authorization tickets" issued by the regiment from soldiers, and weekly medical inspection requirements of the women.

      It also includes expected conduct of soldiers specifying ***"No drunks, no food or drinks allowed, no fighting, no violence against the women allowed."*** The rates were: Officers, one hour, 3 yen; NCO, 30 minutes, 1 yen 30 sen; Soldiers, 30 minutes, 1 yen.

      h. Journal of 39th Independent Motor Battalion, 4th Company, dated May 30, 1942. Location: Batavia, Indonesia.

      "Rules Concerning Control of Venereal Disease.

      "Article 1. The only occasion when contact is permitted with comfort women is when all else fails. (Yamu o ezaru bai ni kagiri).

      "Article 2. When contact is made with comfort women, be sure to use "sack" and also 'seimitsuko' (a venereal disease preventive salve) and immediately after contact sterilize your privates.

      "After contact with comfort women, within three hours report back to the garrison and go to the dispensary, make the necessary report in registration book and receive an inspection by the doctor on duty.

"Thereafter receive an inspection of private parts once a week without fail.

"Those who failed to make a report within three hours after contact and get venereal disease will in addition to being punished be reported to the local mayor." [It is not clear what this report to the local mayor is all about.]

i.. Other Japanese Military Records.

(1) Burma. In 1996, Hirofumi Hayashi gave presentations in England on the subject of comfort women in SE Asia. To quote one part: *"According to Japanese Military documents which I found at the Imperial War Museum, and which is the only document relating to comfort women in Burma, there were 9 comfort houses in Mandalay, 1 of which was Japanese, 1 Guandong-Chinese, 3 Korean, 4 Burmese."* There is no mention on how the women had been recruited.

(2) Numerous military small unit journals are available with comments related to comfort women but are generally the same. **There is not a single document that makes mention of any order or directive that authorizes or legitimizes comfort women being forced to work at a comfort station, held as prisoners for sexual purposes, or of any comfort woman providing sexual service without compensation.**

G. KOREAN ORIGINAL SOURCE DOCUMENTS

1. There are no Korean military documents since Korea was part of Japan. However, a number of original documents relating to the comfort women do exist. One web site contains old Korean newspaper articles reporting on arrests of forced recruitment by Koreans of Korean girls and women as comfort women. However, its validity cannot be confirmed.

2. Diary of a Korean who managed a comfort station. In 2013, a book, <u>Diary of a Japanese Military Brothel Owner</u>, was published in Korea, which was cited by the translator and others as evidence of forced military recruitment of Korean women by the Japanese military. Korean Professor Choe Kil-sung analyzed this diary. This analysis is available in English and some extracts follow with direct quotes in italics. The writer of the diary, a Mr. Bak, managed comfort stations in Burma and Singapore. The authenticity of the diary has not been questioned by either the Korean government or scholars.

    a. The professor explains his approach to reading the book

"Before I read the book, I had made the decision that I would think about it in a purely objective manner, not for the purpose of reconciliation, peace, or understanding between Korea and Japan. In other words, I would read it without taking into consideration the political rights or wrongs of colonialism, nationalism, pacifism, and other –isms.

"One must bear in mind that research is not possible if one starts with the presumption that colonialism is absolutely evil. *Most of the now-independent nations of Asia, Africa, Latin America, and Oceania were colonies of the Western powers at some point in the past. Likewise, parts of Asia were colonized by the Japanese, but no matter how bad one might think that was, a researcher should simply treat facts as facts.*

"The problem is that, in South Korea, Japanese colonialism is regarded as the root of all evil and South Koreans still will not discuss the reality and consequences of Japanese rule. *By its very nature, scholarship must be free from the shackles of nationalism and patriotism. This is what 'academic freedom' is all about…."*

    b. The professor's analysis.

In writing the diary, Mr. Bak acknowledges himself to be a loyal subject of the Japanese Empire. In the…he writes about the 'Holy War for East Asia,' 'the long life of the Emperor and the prosperity of the imperial family,' and 'blessing the nation with prosperity and the Imperial Army with martial fortune.' I suspect that this represents how Koreans at the time viewed their country. The concept of 'holy war' and the 'Imperial Army' advocated within the Japanese

Empire had taken root in the minds of Koreans as well, who apparently saw themselves as 'loyal imperial subjects.'"

The professor describes the work and daily life of the diary writer, Mr. Bak. Among those activities include, *"submitting the employment permits of comfort women."* Mr. Bak seemed will paid, spent lavishly, *"buying expensive suits, shoes, watches"* and even purchased a car.

The professor: *"One might ask what kind of position Mr. Bak must have had to be living this kind of life, and yet it appears that he was just the manager of a comfort station, organizing and administering things at the front desk, and not a soldier or a civilian employee of the Japanese Army. **Indeed he seemed wary of military employees and always thought of his business as being independent from the men of the army.**"*

"I went out to eat with army-affiliated civilians, but, starting from tomorrow, I won't be able to eat there anymore. (Diary entry of January 12, 1944)."

"I went to have dinner at...with ..., but was told only soldiers and civilian military employees were allowed to enter.... (Diary entry of April 23, 1943)."

"One can understand from such entries that a separation exists between military employees and comfort station manager. Evidently, based on this account the comfort women were likewise not employees of the military.

*"Even though the comfort women business was not a part of the military, **it did have a tight connection with the military**. Perhaps, upon reflection, it would be fair to say that the military and the comfort stations were in a 'special relationship.' Alternatively, one might say that the comfort stations were governed by the military administering the territories occupied by the Japanese Army.*

*"In addition, **although the diary mentions many people bearing Japanese-style names, in most cases these were Japanese-style names taken by ethnic Koreans.**"*

The professor's comments on the military's control.

"The relationship between the comfort stations and the military comes to light whenever the Japanese Army was on the move, but it is not clear whether the comfort stations transferred along with an army regiment on the their own volition or under military order."

The professor reviewed a number of diary entries relating to movement of comfort stations with the military including one where they were ordered to, *"but I heard **the comfort women were all resolutely opposed to it and would not go**. (Dairy entry of March 10, 1943)."* The professor's conclusion was that *"**it would appear from statement like these that comfort stations were not appendages of the military**."*

There are numerous diary entries that clearly establishes that Mr. Bak, the diary writer, was not part of the military but an independent businessman, engaging in other businesses besides managing comfort stations.

The professor comments that, *"When Mr. Bak transferred to a new location he utilized the standard means of transportation, usually train, boats, cars, and carriages. The fact that he had to 'hitch a ride' on military-use vehicles proves that he was not a soldier."*

He continues: *"What's more, because he was not a soldier, he had no choice but to rely on civilian facilities even for the accommodations where he stayed during the transfer. For his meals he likewise made do with what his friends and acquaintances provided to him at their homes."* However, at times Mr. Bak would go to see the logistic department of the military and ask for lodging for the night. The Japanese would treat him nicely, but for long stays he would seek out friends.

The professor had this to say about comfort stations:

"The truth about the comfort stations.

"In the late nineteenth century, Japanese prostitutes, known as karayuki san, exported the sex trade abroad, especially in the vicinity of eastern and southeastern Asia. For instance, it well known that the typical red light districts were established by Chinese and Japanese prostitutes in Singapore. However, Mr. Bak does not mention this topic in his diary.

"Apart from comfort stations run by Koreans, there were also other comfort stations in the area of Arakan, including those run by Japanese and those run by residents of Arakan described as 'local people comfort stations' in a diary entry of June 18, 1943...."

"Now that they were subjects of the Japanese Empire, this was probably the first time that Koreans were going abroad to do business. The diary makes it clear that several Koreans had wide-ranging business contacts in places like Indonesia, Malaysia, Thailand, and East Timor, and in addition to comfort stations they operated a diverse range of businesses, including restaurants, cafeterias, rice cake shops, confectionaries, tofu dealerships, and oil refineries.

"When people think of a comfort station, there are probably quite a few who instantly imagine a military camp or an army tent. And yet, it seems that, for the most part, the comfort stations were actually located in ordinary civilian buildings. Furthermore, it would appear that they were not segregated into designated red-light districts."

"These comfort stations were also engaged in buying and selling, borrowing and loaning, and transfers of property."

At the conclusion of the analyses, the Professor had this to say:

"After I read the diary the first time, I concluded definitely that the comfort stations were not military institutions, but rather similar to wartime brothels. I wrote about this... in September 2014.

"Despite this, the translator of the book Professor An Byeong-jik received the exact opposite impression. Professor An argues that Mr. Bak's diary proves that the Japanese Army gave the comfort station managers and the comfort women a status akin to Japanese military employees, integrated them into a subordinate branch of the military hierarchy, and unilaterally ordered them onto the frontlines. These claims were given a great deal of sensational coverage by the South Korean media, and that was the way everyone in Korea accepted the diary. In other words, the diary was 'definitive evidence' for the forcible mobilization of comfort women by the Japanese Army, quite contrary to what I had taken from it.

"My areas of interest are certainly not limited to the current status of Japan-Korea relations or specifically to politics and the national interests of one country or another. Even so, I do feel that my readers and I have arrived at a good opportunity to confront these issues, so it is natural that my interest would be directed here. However, what I desire is not to analyze such problems on a superficial level, but rather to seek out the truth that lies below the surface. This is my primary concern and is the message that I want to have heard. I suppose that I have taken advantage of this opportunity so that my message will be understood sympathetically.

"Undoubtedly, the military and the comfort stations enjoyed close relations, but that alone does not allow us to conclude that the military controlled them. Though the diary was called 'Diary of a Japanese Military Brothel Manager,' after reading it, I somehow felt the urge to remove the words 'Japanese Military' from the title."

This ends the analysis of the diary.

H. CONCLUDING REMARKS

Contrary to our system of justice, Japan has been found guilty in a court of public opinion of abducting 200,000 women for sex slaves based on unproven allegations. In effect, Japan is in a position of having to prove a negative. This compilation provides evidence the allegations are without merit. Just as My Lai is not "proof" that it was the policy of U.S. Forces to massacre innocent Vietnamese civilians, a few cases of involuntary prostitution is not "proof" comfort women were abducted sex slaves. There is no evidence even of the existence of 200,000 comfort women. From the records, the total number of comfort women is estimated at less than a tenth of that.

Many see this as a human rights issue without questioning the truth of the allegations. Japan accepted full responsibility for WWII in Asia, offered up its entire citizenry for war crimes trials, paid reparations, purged former military officers from public office, carried out numerous reforms, and adopted a constitution to never again engage in war. Today, Japan is one of the most, if not the most, democratic and peace loving of all the nations. Its aid to developing countries around the world is exceeded only by the United States. While that does not excuse war crimes committed by Japan, neither does Japan deserve to be demonized for crimes it did not commit.

The image of Japan being "absolutely evil" was implanted in the minds of Americans during WWII. Perhaps this was deserved, perhaps not, but it provided a convenient rationalization for the atomic bombing of Japanese civilians in that war by placing the blame entirely on the Japanese themselves. This perception of "evil Japan" has continued to this day. Most Americans believe the Japanese military raped and looted its way across Asia. Thus, any allegation against Japan's conduct during WWII, even without evidence, is readily accepted as the truth.

Since the end of WWII, Japan has maintained a low posture in dealing with other nations. It has quietly accepted the meddling of other nations into its internal affairs. No other nation has been subjected to the scrutiny and criticism that Japan has endured to this day. No other nation would allow foreigners to dictate what is taught in schools or who is honored at national cemeteries. Japan has quietly tolerated these intrusions into its sovereignty without complaint.

In 1951, the peace treaty ending WWII was signed and all signatories agreed the war was over and settled. Japan has lived up to the terms of the treaty. There is no clause in the peace treaty that requires Japan to apologize forever. Even then, Japan would probably acknowledge any unsettled past wrongdoing. However, no nation should have to apologize for wrongdoing which did not occur. Even Germany did not do that. The comfort women issue has caused a subtle (dramatic?) change in Japan. It seems Japan has finally decided enough is enough! For the first time, rather than quietly accepting an insulting breach of international protocol by the erection by Koreans of a comfort woman statue in front of its consulate in Pusan, Japan reacted by recalling its ambassador. After suffering insults all these years, has Japan finally realized that seeking resolution with a country that disregards international agreements is futile? The comfort women issue has in fact had an opposite effect of that contemplated. Instead of humbling Japan, the false allegations have in effect awakened Japan from feeling a necessity to meekly endure unwarranted bullying.

These WWII documents, while proving the allegations to be without merit, raise questions about why advocates are so intent on smearing Japan's reputation with the American public and around the world. On the surface it might appear to be a human rights issue but in reality is something far more sinister with a political purpose. One of the main organizations driving this is Chong Dae Hyup, a South Korean organization with North Korean connections. Its purpose is to use the comfort women issue to generate anti-Japan sentiment. The isolation of Japan will mean the isolation of the U.S. from NE Asia. A Korean website reported a 1992 meeting in Pyongyang, North Korea, when that decision was made. While that has not been confirmed, from about that time the comfort women issue gained momentum. Here in the U.S., this movement is mainly driven by Koreans and the China lobby. Most Americans do not realize they are being manipulated and have never heard of Chong Dae Hyup and the China lobby.

Many Americans think of Japan only as a former enemy and that a rearmed Japan would be a threat to world peace. Today, Japan is not the Japan of WWII, it is a democracy and our most essential and reliable ally. In addition to being located in a geographically strategic location, Japan has the third largest economy in the world. Even with its peace constitution, Japan's defense budget is in the top ten in the world, stressing quality over quantity. With the exception of China and Korea, Japan is regarded favorably by most nations. This is especially true in SE Asia, India, the Middle East and Africa. Our close alliance has endured for over seventy years based on mutual trust, friendship and common belief in democracy. We must not be duped into supporting activists bent on undermining this relationship. The strategic impact of the abrogation of the U.S./Japan military alliance on the United States would be incalculable.

We must not teach our children to hate Japan; history yes, but not unfounded allegations. Hate will only generate more hate and tear our alliance apart. Japan does not teach its children to hate. As an example, at the base of a mountain a few miles north and inland from the coastal city of Nakatsu in southern Japan, there is a beautiful park built in memory of American crew members of a B-29 that crashed at that site. At the entrance is a large monument listing the names and the diagrams of the home states of each crew member. The B-29 was rammed by a Japanese fighter pilot but there is no monument for the Japanese pilot, only the Americans. This park was built to honor the Americans.

To the Japanese, the park is nothing special but few Americans would be able to visit the site without eyes watering. This B-29 had just dropped its bombs on Japanese cities, killing countless civilians. Instead of treating it as a war crime to be remembered for a thousand years, the crew members are honored and remembered, not as enemies, but as brave young men who gave their lives for their country at this far away place. This park tells more about the Japanese people than all the temples of Kyoto and Nara.

The comfort women issue has had a serious effect on relations between Korea and Japan. It changed Japanese attitudes from a record high of popularity of all things Korean to a dismal low during the tenure of past president Park Geun-hye. Her berating of Japan on the comfort women issue even led to anti-Korean demonstrations and hate speeches in Japan, something unheard of since the Tokyo earthquake of almost a century ago. The negative economic impact on Korea because of anti-Korean sentiment in Japan has not been insignificant. The effect on security cooperation has also suffered.

This report did not cover the Women's Volunteer Labor Corps (*teishintai* in Japanese, *chongsindae* in Korean) system used to mobilize young unemployed women in Japan and Korea for factory work during the final years of WWII. It is cited by many as proof of government recruitment of comfort women. The Japan Policy Institute (Nihon Seisaku Kenkyu Center) published a detailed report in 2015 on how false information about the Women's Volunteer Labor Force was used to fuel allegations of official government involvement in the forced recruitment of comfort women.

By August, 1944, when the Women's Volunteer Labor Corps was initiated, Japan was fighting for survival. By mid-1942, Japan had lost at the battle of Midway and from that point was fighting a defensive war. By 1943, comfort women were being evacuated from the war zones. By the time the Teishintai system was initiated, Japan was being subjected to constant aerial bombardment. Yet, many Koreans continue to believe the system was used to recruit involuntary comfort women.

The difference in the attitudes of Koreans and Taiwanese toward Japan is striking. Taiwan came under Japanese domination ten years before Korea. Today, the Taiwanese consider Japan as their most admired country, greatly outdistancing even the U.S. in popularity. [Sakai, Toru. Chu Kan Igai Mina Shin Nichi (Other than China/Korea – All Japan Friendly), p.18.] It is interesting that while many Taiwanese believe that forced recruitment of Taiwanese women did take place and recently opened a comfort women museum in Taipei, the majority still love Japan.

From all the evidence in military records, the concluding remarks of Professor Choe Kil-sung's analysis of the diary of a Korean manager of comfort stations sums up the comfort women issue very well. It is repeated here:

"UNDOUBTEDLY, THE MILITARY AND THE COMFORT STATIONS ENJOYED CLOSE RELATIONS, BUT THAT ALONE DOES NOT ALLOW US TO CONCLUDE THAT THE MILITARY CONTROLLED THEM."

- End –

LIST OF WWII REPORTS/DOCUMENTS

A. U.S. and Allied Reports

    1. HQ, Island Command, Guam, Serial No. 846, May 12, 1945.

    2. U.S. Pacific Command and Pacific Fleet, U.S. Military Commission Order No. 11 (undated).

    3. U.S. Office of War Information, Psychological Warfare Team Interrogation Report No. 49, Oct 1, 1944.

    4. Headquarters U.S. I Corps, 163d Language Detachment Report No. 163LD-1 0223, "Combined Enemy Preliminary Report," dated 23 May 1945.

    5. U.S. Military Intelligence Service, Captured Personnel & Material Branch report, dated 24 April, 1945, of three Korean civilian employees of the Japanese Navy

    6. ATIS (Allied Translator Interpreter Sections) Research Report No. 120, "Amenities of the Japanese Armed Forces," 15 Nov 45.

    7. ATIS Interrogation Report No. 60, 17 Apr 43.

    8. ATIS Interrogation Report No. 63, 19 Apr 43.

    9. ATIS Interrogation Report No. 78, 15 May 43.

    10. ATIS Interrogation Report No. 94, 15 Jun 43.

    11. ATIS Interrogation Report No. 104, 27 Jun 43.

    12. ATIS Interrogation Report No. 577, 23 Jan 45.

    13. OSS (Office of Strategic Service) India-Burma Theater, Memo D-57, 15 June 1945, Subject: "Interrogation of Indian National Army Prisoner from Molmein," by OSS Det 404. [National Archives Record SSG 236 Box 80 Folder 1370].

    14. OSS Memorandum by Dr. Schofield, undated, Subject: Interrogation of Japanese PW for Psychological Warfare." [National Archives SSG 226 Box 88 Folder 1596]

    15. Interagency Working Group Final Report to U.S. Congress on Nazi War Crimes & Japanese Imperial Government Records in the National Archives, 2007.

B. Dutch Reports

    1. The Bart von Poelgeest Report, "Report of a Study of Dutch Government Documents on the Forced Prostitution of Dutch Women in the Dutch East Indies during the Japanese Occupation."

    2. War Crimes Evidentiary Document No. 5591, Jun 7, 1946.

    3. War Crimes Evidentiary Document No. 1330, Jul 5, 1946.

    4. NEFIS (Netherlands Forces Intelligence Service) Report No. 422, 23 Oct 43.

    5. NEFIS Report 27 Dec 44, "Compilation of NEFIS Rpt Nos. 450, 538, 553, 555, 580, 583, 585, 589, and 593."

    6. NEFIS Report, 6 Dec 44, "Compilation of NEFIS Rpt Nos. 534, 552, 567, 568, 579, 586, 587, 588, and 592."

    7. NEFIS Report, 6 Nov 44, "Compilation of NEFIS Rpt Nos. 455-469."

    8. NEFIS Report, 29 Oct 44, "Compilation of NEFIS Rpt Nos. 366-378, 404-407, 410-417."

    9. NEFIS Report, 6 Nov 44, "Compilation of NEFIS Rpt Nos. 455-469."

    10. NEFIS Report, 21 Dec 44, "Compilation of NEFIS Rpt Nos. 450, 538, 553, 555, 580, 583, 585, 589-593."

11. NEFIS Report, 10 Jan 45, "Compilation of NEFIS Rpt Nos. 818, 820-888."

12. NEFIS Report, 27 Jan 45, "Compilation of NEFIS Rpt Nos. 886, 887, 888."

13. NEFIS Report, 7 Feb 45, "Compilation of NEFIS Rpt Nos. 997-1005."

14. NEFIS Report No. 1244, 9 Mar 45.

15. NEFIS Report, 5 May 45, "Compilation of NEFIS Rpt Nos. 1590-1630."

16. NEFIS Report No. 751, 31 Dec 44,

17. NEFIS Report, 23 Mar 45, "Compilation of NEFIS Rpt Nos. 1235-1238."

18. NEFIS Report No. 1252, 10 May 45.

19. NEFIS Report, 12 Feb 45, "Compilation of NEFIS Rpt Nos. 1066, 1196-1253."

C. Australian Documents

1. Gordon Thomas Diary. Daily diary of events in Rabaul during Japanese occupation. (Thomas, Prisoners in Rabaul: Civilians in Captivity 1942-1945).

2. D.C.S. Sissons, "The Australian War Crimes Trials and Independence, 1942-1951."

D. Japanese Government and Military Documents.

1. The following translated documents in ATIS Report No. 120.

a. "Rules for Authorized Restaurants and Houses of Prostitution," Feb 43, Manila.

b. Manila Air Depot Regulations on Use of Brothels, Aug 44 to Oct 44.

c. Regulations governing special brothels in Shanghai Area.

d. "Tacloban Brothel Regulations," undated.

e. Mimeographed document titled, "Brothel Regulations," dated Aug 44.

f. Japanese Navy Regulations concerning Brothels in Rabaul.

2. The following Japanese documents were not available in English:

a. Japanese Consul Generals' Reports to Foreign Minister of Japan on Status of Countrymen (Japanese, Korean, Taiwanese) and Businesses (including comfort stations) in Chinese Cities.

(1) Jiujiang, Central China, Report No. 561, Nov 8, 1938.

(2) Nanchang, Central China, Report No. 217, Aug 9, 1939.

(3) Chiaohu, Central China, Report No. 170, Aug 2, 1939.

b. Governor General of Taiwan's Report on Kwantung

c. Japanese Military Documents:

(1) Army Department Directive, Mar 4, 1938.

(2) Army Department Directive No. 1955, Sep 4, 1940.

(3) North China Area Army Directive, Jul 14, 1938.

(4) North China, 3d Mountain Artillery Regt Regulation, Oct 1940.

(5) North China, Independent Siege Heavy Artillery, 2d Battalion Internal Regulations, Mar 16, 1938.

(6) N China, 14th Division, Medical Company Journal, Nov 1938.

(7) Batavia, East Indies, 39th Independent Motor Battalion, 4th Company Journal, May 30, 1942.

E. Korean Documents

Choe, Kil-sung, Professor, "Analysis of Diary of Comfort Station Manager."

Made in the USA
San Bernardino, CA
05 June 2019